THE BOOK OF
CALM

THE BOOK OF
CALM

*Relaxing ways to
manage stress*

Aurum Press

Contents

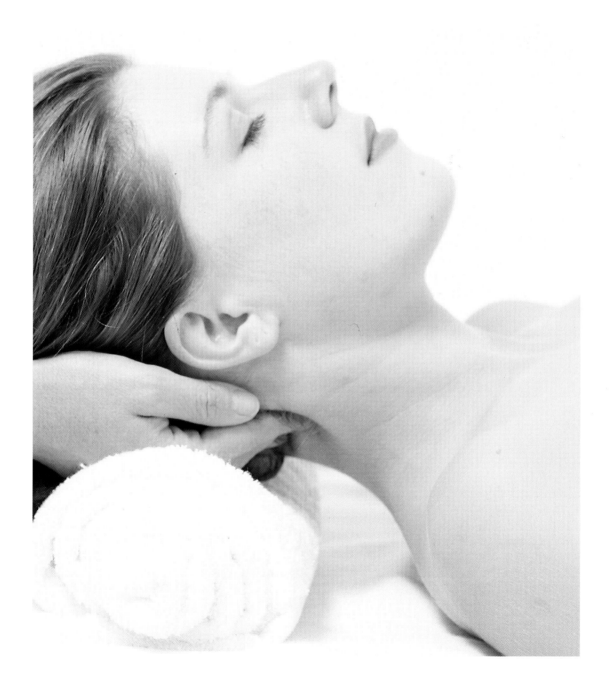

The Way to Calm

Relaxation is a state of being that seems elusive to many of us.
We live life at a hectic pace with many demands and responsibilities.
Stress is not always negative and is an important part of our lives;
but for most of us the balance between relaxation and stress has been lost.

Under stress our muscles contract, adrenaline is released into the bloodstream, our hearts begin to beat faster and our blood pressure increases; we breathe more quickly, our metabolism speeds up, and we sweat to keep cool. This "fight or flight" response is entirely appropriate if we are in danger, if we are about to compete or if we need to spring into action. However, our bodies react in this way, in varying degrees, to all stressful situations. If the day is a series of stressful events, providing no opportunity to release the built-up tension and energy, the body does not have time to return to a "normal" state.

When we are in a relaxed state, the rate of our heartbeat and blood pressure is lower, we breathe more slowly, our muscles are less tense and our metabolism slows down.

In a *deeply* relaxed state, our brain wave patterns reduce in frequency. From the beta waves of our everyday conscious state, they move to the slower alpha waves of a relaxed state, then to the even slower theta waves of a deeply relaxed state. In this state our minds are alert yet calm and peaceful. Our metabolism, heart rate and breathing become even slower as we become more relaxed.

Our bodies use less oxygen and expel less carbon dioxide; our hormones return to a balanced state and blood lactate levels are reduced. Our internal organs work more effectively and, although blood pressure reduces, circulation improves with more blood reaching the extremities of the body. Our muscles become soft and loose, and we become more aware of our bodies and feelings and less aware of our surroundings. Both our minds and bodies are rested in the process of relaxing deeply.

*Deep relaxation is a completely different state
from just socializing with friends
or lying in front of the television.*

It is important to be aware of how the different ways in which we choose to relax affect us. Not all recreational activities will leave us in a deeply relaxed state. For instance, we may enjoy watching television, seeing a film or reading a book. These activities can expand our way of seeing the world, challenging or reinforcing our beliefs; they also provide entertainment and information. They do not, however, encourage deep relaxation as television, films and books stimulate the mind — our bodies may even react to events in the stories as if we were physically involved. Having a drink or a cup of coffee with friends provides an opportunity for self-expression, social interaction, and a sharing of common interests. This is an activity we may greatly enjoy, yet it is not a deeply relaxing experience. Meetings with friends often take place in noisy, smoky environments where we are likely to consume caffeine or alcohol; all of these factors place stress on our bodies.

The key is to find a balance between work, leisure pursuits and relaxation. Spending even a small amount of time each day in a deeply relaxed state will benefit your health and well-being. The effects of living primarily in a relaxed state or primarily in a stressed state are very pronounced. When we are relaxed, we are more likely to think clearly and be aware of what is happening around us; we are also likely to be more conscious of how we are responding to those events. High levels of energy enable us to experience unexpected events as opportunities and challenges full of possibilities. At work, we can expect to utilize time more effectively; the day will also seem to flow at a more even pace. The ability to focus makes us more efficient. When we are relaxed, we experience greater enjoyment in everything we do. Sleep is more regular, deep and peaceful, and we usually awake feeling refreshed and vital. Finding regular time for relaxation leads to an overall improvement in our health. And if we do become ill, we are more likely to recover quickly, as relaxation encourages the body to regain its normal self-regulation.

When we are stressed, we feel overwhelmed by the pressures of life. The list of problems appears endless. We never seem to enjoy ourselves because we are always thinking of work to be done, of the money we don't have, or the list of things that should have been done. Falling asleep may be difficult because we are unable to switch off. We may wake frequently during the night or have disturbing dreams. This stress behavior will cause our health to deteriorate; we may become more susceptible to colds, flu, and headaches.

A stressed state of being and a relaxed state of being are both self-perpetuating. To a certain extent, both are based on habit. Being stressed leads to repetitive behavior that creates stress. For example: We come home from a long day at work and the temptation is to kick off our shoes, slump into a chair and watch TV. As a repeated pattern, this behavior increases the stress in our lives. By contrast, the benefit we can feel from regularly practicing some short, simple relaxation techniques, and being aware of our diet and environment, is palpable. These positive effects become in themselves the motivation to increase the time we spend in deep relaxation. Thus our stress levels are reduced even further, and we soon find ourselves moving from a stress cycle to a relaxation cycle.

Symptoms of being stressed

When we are stressed over a long period of time, without the opportunity to release this tension, symptoms will appear. These vary from person to person but some common signs of too much stress are:

- Difficulty in falling asleep
- Waking frequently during the night
- Headaches
- Backache
- Indigestion and other digestive problems
- High blood pressure
- Poor co-ordination
- Shallow breathing and tightness in the chest
- Rapid speech
- Short temper
- General feelings of frustration, anger, anxiety, tearfulness, and mood swings
- Increased number of arguments with friends or family

Take notice of the environment in which you live and work,
and take action to reduce or eliminate those elements
you feel may be creating stress in your life.

Stressors

To achieve a state of calm it is first necessary to identify the causes of stress. Many external causes of stress may be minimized or avoided once you become aware of them.

The relaxation techniques described in this book may be useful tools in changing your methods of dealing with stress in your life. The techniques are intended to be simple and practical, and suitable to be undertaken by you at home. However, if you have been stressed for a long period of time, or if your health is being affected by your stress levels, it would be wise to discuss your situation with a health professional.

Some common stressors are:

Emotional and mental

- Death of someone you love
- Divorce or the end of a significant relationship
- Birth of a child
- Change of job or career
- Moving house
- Deadlines and new projects
- Traveling long distances
- Any sort of major change in your routine

Environment

- Lack of fresh air and space — if you live in the city both of these factors may be difficult to overcome. Spend some time discovering your local parks or gardens.
- Noise — sharp intermittent noises can trigger a "fight or flight" response; so too can low continual noise like that emitted by air conditioning units, and the low rumble of heavy traffic or office equipment.

Diet

- Caffeine — taken in large amounts, caffeine can cause irritability, anxiety, and restlessness. If you feel you are consuming too many caffeine drinks — coffee, tea, and cola — cut back gradually. If you don't want to give them up all together, try limiting your intake to one or two drinks a day.

- Alcohol — over the years there has been conflicting evidence as to whether regular, moderate alcohol intake is detrimental to your health. More than moderate intake, however, is almost sure to cause problems and will place an added stress on your body. Be aware that heavy drinking can also be a symptom of stress.

Habits

- Smoking — apart from the many other medical hazards it causes, smoking reduces the amount of oxygen taken into the lungs, which immediately creates a stressful state. Contact a health professional for information on the various options available to you if you smoke and would like to give up.

Quick Calm

Rather than letting the stress cycle build, it is better to deal with minor stress quickly and effectively when it arises.

A daily routine of relaxation techniques is the most effective way to avoid becoming highly stressed. If you know that you are about to face a stressful situation, there is a variety of "quick" techniques that can assist you in staying relaxed and calm.

Take a moment to notice

When you realize you're becoming stressed, take a moment to notice what your body is doing. How is your posture? Are your shoulders relaxed? Have you been holding your breath? Which parts of your body are tense? What is causing the stress? Is the stress necessary? In identifying which areas of your body you have tensed, you will probably find you have already relaxed them. If not, use one of the "quick tip" exercises to release the tension. If you are able to isolate the cause of the stress and you discover the stress is unnecessary, see what you can do to change the situation or your reaction to it. This way you can proceed in a relaxed state.

Smile and laugh

The age-old adage of "laughter is the best medicine" is particularly true if you're in a stressed state. A smile or a laugh can break the stress cycle and give you a different perspective on life.

The next time you feel anxious over your workload, or there's a day when everything that could go wrong has gone wrong, try to mentally take a step back and ask yourself whether being stressed and stern about it is going to improve the stituation.

If you can recognize you are not going to lose time by smiling and perhaps even being able to laugh at yourself for being so serious you have taken a step twoards relaxation.

A good laugh releases endorphins into our bodies and improves how we feel both physically and psychologically. Spend some time discovering what makes you smile and what makes you laugh, and keep a few triggers handy. These could be a book of cartoons, a comic video, or even some mental images you can call to mind. The added bonus is that smiling and laughter are infectious, so by lightening your own day you can also lighten the day of those around you.

Sing

Singing is an effective way to release emotional tension, and is especially useful if you are anxious or fearful. It helps the body relax as it increases circulation and can trigger the release of endorphins by the brain. Don't be concerned about singing in tune and sing whatever type of music you like, either solo or accompanied by a recording. If you don't know the words, make them up or even make nonsensical sounds. If singing feels too boisterous, start by humming a tune and work your way into a song. Use this technique wherever you like, in the car or the shower.

Shake out the tension

This effective exercise is particularly useful in a work situation. Find a private spot in which you can practice — it only takes a minute or two.

Firstly, stretch upward inhaling deeply, then let your breath out with a "ha," flop your upper body over at the waist and let your arms hang loosely downward. Lift each shoulder alternately to "shake out" tension in the shoulders and upper back, and slowly nod your head to release tension in the neck muscles.

Stand upright again and take two or three deep breaths, focusing on releasing any remaining tension. Create a mental image of yourself staying calm and relaxed throughout the day.

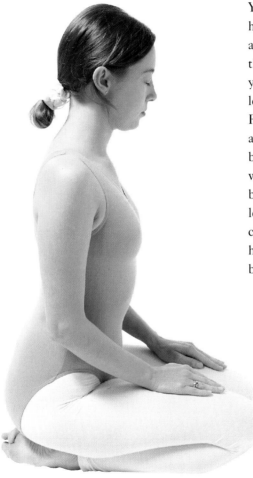

Five-minute meditation

You can practice this technique at home, at work, sitting in the park — anywhere you like. Sit comfortably on the floor or in a chair, making sure your back is straight, your hands lying loosely in your lap. Close your eyes. Focus on your breath moving slowly in and out of your body. Each time you breathe in, imagine yourself filling with vitality and energy. As you breathe out, imagine all the tension leaving your body. Do not become concerned if stray thoughts enter your head during this meditation, simply bring your focus back to your breath.

Desk stretch

You can try this short stretching routine at your desk. It's a great relaxation technique to use just before you go into an important meeting or before making that phone call you've been putting off. It is also effective if you are starting to feel stressed and tight around the back and shoulders, and don't have time to get away from your desk. It only takes a few minutes to complete and will leave you feeling refreshed and centered.

1. Push your chair back until, with your back against the chair, you are at an arm's length from the desk. Sit squarely in your chair with your legs shoulder width apart and your feet flat on the floor. Close your eyes and take two or three slow, deep breaths.

2. Clasp your hands behind your back and gradually lean backwards, arching your upper back over the top of the chair. Return to the position in step 1 and take two or three deep breaths.

3. Place your palms against the edge of the desk and, keeping your back straight, press against the desk as if you were trying to push it away. Hold for a few seconds, then let go. This will tighten and then relax the muscles in your arms and chest. Return to the position in step 1 and take two or three deep breaths.

4. Placing your legs together, tighten your thigh muscles and lift your legs until they are straight out in front of you with your toes flexed back toward your body. Hold for a few seconds, then relax. Return to the position in step 1 and take two or three deep breaths.

After-Work Wind Down

Work problems are among the greatest contributors to stress, but the concerns of your job should not impact on your enjoyment of the rest of your life. You can learn to leave work behind.

Many of us lead hectic work lives. We travel to and from work, and juggle home responsibilities, work pressures, and financial commitments. It is not surprising we might find it difficult to switch off at the end of the day.

One technique to overcome this is to create a ritual for yourself that indicates your working day has finished and your recreational time has begun. The ritual doesn't have to be dramatic or formal, just an indication you have moved from one part of the day to another. It may consist of lighting an aromatherapy burner, or changing your clothes and shoes to something loose and comfortable; the ritual may simply consist of standing in the garden for a few moments while enjoying the evening sky. Whatever you choose, keep the ritual simple and use it each day to signify the beginning of your relaxation time.

Incorporate variety into your relaxation time — a relaxation technique will lose its effectiveness if it becomes boring or begins to feel like a chore. Find out what you enjoy most and what works best for you at particular times, giving attention to your mind, your body, and your emotional well-being.

A calming technique for the body

Use a series of stretching exercises or yoga exercises every day after work. This will help your body release the tensions stored during the day and allow your muscles to relax. As your fitness and stamina increase, you may like to follow up with a long walk, a dance class one or two evenings a week, or a game of tennis or golf on the weekend.

A calming technique for the mind

Practice a meditation, visualization or breathing exercise every day. Even if it is only for ten minutes each day, it can make a great difference in how you feel and how you sleep. If you spend most of your day indoors, try doing this exercise outside; the fresh air can also help you feel revitalized.

A calming technique for the emotions

Do something you really enjoy and that will make you feel uplifted. This can be as simple as curling up in your favorite armchair reading a good book, or taking a long, relaxing bath. You may even like to take up a peaceful but specialized hobby, like growing orchids in a hot house. Another enjoyable and relaxing experience is taking the time to have a leisurely talk with an old friend.

Bedtime Preparation

*Draw yourself a warm
to hot bath and add some
aromatherapy oils. Play some
relaxing music, lie back in the
water, and breathe deeply ...*

A bath is a wonderful way to end the day and prepare yourself for bed. Ensure you have done everything you need to do before your bath, then pamper yourself. Try a luxurious bubble bath every now and then, if this appeals, and experiment with different oil combinations. You may like to practice some visualizations in the bath, or a mini-meditation. Often, after a bath like this, sleep will descend upon you moments after you go to bed.

If you have difficulty getting to sleep because your mind keeps racing, avoid doing anything mentally stimulating in the hour before you go to bed. Try a meditation in preference to reading a book. Give yourself a massage instead of watching television, and use this time to calm your mind. Don't drink any alcohol or caffeine during the evening; instead, try a hot chamomile or lavender tea.

Bedtime relaxation exercise

The following tense-relax exercise, performed while you are lying in bed, is a simple way of relaxing before sleep.

1. Lie flat on your back with your arms beside you. Take a few deep breaths and imagine all tension leaving your body.

2. Beginning at your feet, flex and tense them as hard as you can, hold for a few seconds and then relax.

3. Point your toes and tighten your calf muscles; hold for a few seconds, then relax.

4. Repeat this process for each set of muscles in your body, working up your legs, to your buttocks, and lower back. Tighten your back muscles by raising your shoulders up to your ears, and then relaxing. Continue this process for your hands, arms, and neck.

5. Finish by pulling a face with your jaw clenched, and then relaxing; and another with your jaw open, and then relaxing.

6. Breathe deeply, keeping your focus on your breath. Check your body for any residual tension and, if you find any, tighten the area and relax once more. With each exhalation, imagine all remaining tension leaving your body.

Deep Relaxation Exercise

This simple exercise requires no special equipment or training,
and can easily be incorporated into your weekly routine.
By focusing on breathing and relaxing the tension in your muscles,
you will feel the stress slip away.

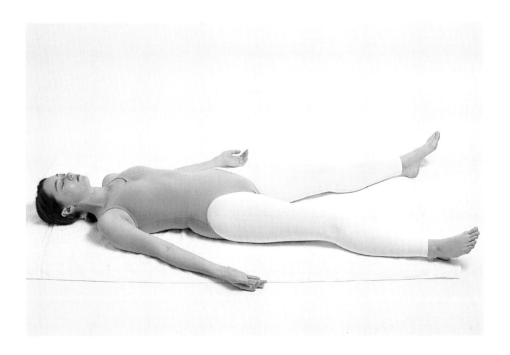

Preparation

Ensure you have 20 to 30 minutes during which you will not be disturbed. Find a place in which you feel comfortable, where the light is soft or dimmed, and that is relatively quiet. Your body temperature may drop during this process, so make sure you are warmly dressed in loose clothing. If you are sensitive to the cold, you may also like to have a blanket or shawl handy to pull over you if necessary. Find a comfortable position. You may lie on your back, your head supported by a pillow, or sit in a chair with your back straight; or you may prefer to sit on the floor, your back against a wall.

The exercise

1. Close your eyes and focus on your breath. Breathe deeply in through your nose to avoid drying out your mouth and throat, and exhale through your mouth. Be aware of how your breath feels as it fills your abdomen, and how it feels as you exhale and your abdomen falls.

2. With each inhalation imagine all the tension in your body collecting together, and with each exhalation imagine all this tension leaving your body. Continue to breathe deeply and evenly.

3. Now move your attention to different parts of your body. Begin with your feet. Let the floor take the full weight of your feet and feel them become heavy. Imagine them being so heavy that you couldn't possibly move them. Now become aware of your legs. They are also becoming heavy, a weight on the floor. If you notice any tension, imagine it being released with each exhalation.

4. Repeat step 3 with your concentration, focusing in turn, on your buttocks, stomach, back, arms, and head. There is no set amount of time for you to relax these areas of your body. Allow as much time as is necessary to feel all tension has left your muscles. Return to an area if you notice tension there at a later time.

Being in a deeply relaxed state for 20 to 30 minutes at least two or three times a week can act as a preventive measure against becoming overly stressed and fatigued. As you practice techniques for becoming deeply relaxed, you will find it easier and quicker to achieve relaxation.

5. Return your attention to your breath. If you find your mind wandering, try not to participate in these stray thoughts; simply observe them before returning your focus to your breath. You will find that, as you become more practiced at relaxation techniques, you will be able to maintain your focus more easily.

6. Bring your attention now to how you feel emotionally, and be aware of any stress you might be feeling. Try to view this stress as being separate from you and from your body. Continue breathing slowly while you observe the stress, and allow it to take on a shape and/or color.

7. When you have established an image of the stress as a separate object, slowly watch it dissolve and flow away with each breath you exhale.

8. Once you feel completely relaxed, allow yourself to stay where you are for as long as feels comfortable. Being in a deeply relaxed state can alter our sense of time. It is not unusual to feel that only a few moments have passed, when in reality you might have been relaxing for 15 or 20 minutes.

9. Give yourself time to slowly return to an ordinary, waking state. You may like to gently stretch some of your muscles while you remain sitting or lying. You should only stand up when you feel ready, and any feelings of weightlessness or disorientation have passed.

Acupressure

*This ancient healing technique can be used safely
and effectively at home to treat the symptoms of stress,
from anxiety and tension to headaches.*

Acupuncture and acupressure have evolved from the Oriental healing arts, which utilize the concepts of "Yin" and "Yang" and of "Ch'i" (or "Qi"). In Chinese philosophy, Yin and Yang represent the polarities of life. In very simple terms, Yin is the passive, feminine, cold aspect, while Yang is the active, masculine, hot aspect. Ch'i is the vital life-force energy that runs through our bodies in channels or "meridians." When we are in good health, Yin and Yang are in balance; body, mind and emotions are in harmony; and the Ch'i flows freely through our body. When an imbalance occurs, acupuncture and acupressure are healing techniques that can be applied to the points along the meridians. They aim to balance the Ch'i and relieve the symptoms of the illness.

An acupuncturist will use a variety of diagnostic techniques, including checking the "pulse" of each meridian to identify where an imbalance of energy is caused. He or she will then insert needles into the relevant points. There are hundreds of different points, each with a different function, so acupuncture should only be practiced by a fully qualified acupuncturist.

Acupressure, however, works with finger pressure on the same points, and while you should not attempt to treat yourself for a serious health problem, you can use acupressure as an effective relaxation technique at home. The individual points are named after the major organ in the corresponding meridian, or after the two "control" meridians followed by a number. The control meridians are known as the "Governing Vessel," which incorporates the spine, and the "Conception Vessel," which runs down the middle of the front of the body.

When to avoid acupressure

There are certain times when acupressure is inappropriate. Do not apply pressure to • scar tissue
• an area where the skin is broken • swollen or inflamed areas • varicose veins

How to apply acupressure

Acupressure can be applied either on bare skin or through loose clothing. Try to maintain a light focus on your breathing throughout, ensuring that it is smooth and even.

There are three different types of pressure applied in acupressure in accordance with the desired change in the Ch'i. If the Ch'i is deficient, it is increased by applying firm, stationary pressure to the acupressure point for one or two minutes. If the Ch'i is blocked, it is dispersed by making firm, circular movements with thumb or fingers at the acupressure point for about one or two minutes. If there is excess Ch'i, it is calmed by placing the hand, palm face down, over the acupressure point and holding it there for one or two minutes.

Acupressure points for releasing tension

Hands

Apply pressure to the fleshy part between your thumb and index finger. It is useful for releasing muscular tension around the neck and shoulders. Use circular movements to disperse the Ch'i.
Caution: Do not use this point during pregnancy.

Head

Press the point at the very top of the head at a midpoint between the ears. Use the pad of your thumb to desperse the Ch'i.
Caution: Do not use this point if you have high blood pressure.

Nose

This point is at the top of the nose, between the eyebrows. Gently disperse the Ch'i at this point with the pad of one of your middle fingers.

Aromatherapy

Essential oils extracted from the seeds, leaves, flowers, barks, gums and roots of plants have been used therapeutically since ancient times. Aromatherapy is the modern day rediscovery of these practices. The use of essential oils can have beneficial effects physically and psychologically, and provide the opportunity for some very pleasant relaxation techniques.

The oils may be used in a variety of ways to help reduce stress and tension. Some are particularly suitable for relaxation and will help induce sleep, while others are rejuvenating and uplifting.

Relaxing essential oils

Chamomile ❦ *Cedarwood* ❦ *Clary Sage*

Frankincense ❦ *Lavender* ❦ *Neroli*

Rose ❦ *Sandalwood* ❦ *Ylang Ylang*

Aromatherapy baths

Baths are often associated with lying back and letting the cares of the day slip away. Being immersed in warm water is in itself relaxing and the use of aromatherapy can make a bath even more effective as a relaxation technique. Your choice of oils should take into account whether you want to be relaxed and alert, ready to carry on with the day, or whether you intend to sleep shortly after your bath. Experiment with the oils to discover which combinations you enjoy and find most effective.

After filling your bath, simply add 4 to 12 drops of the oil or combination of oils you have selected and agitate the water to disperse the oil through the bath so that it does not cause irritation to your skin. Or you may like to use a commercial bath lotion or soap that contains suitable essential oils.

To take full advantage of the effects of an aromatherapy bath, it is worth spending a little time in preparation. Make sure you will not be disturbed for 20 to 30 minutes and that you have your thickest, fluffiest towel or a toweling bathrobe ready. A few candles will provide a warm glow of light, and relaxation music will add to the effect (see MUSIC, pages 68–71). Ensure you will be comfortable, with a "bath pillow" or rolled towel to support your head, and make the decision that this time is just for you and only for relaxation.

For a relaxing bath before bed

The water should be as hot as is comfortable.
This will help your muscles relax and encourage
the pores in your skin to open, allowing
absorption of the aromatherapy oils. The heat will
also vaporize the oils, making inhalation possible.
A few oil combination suggestions are:

Bergamot 6 drops
Lavender 3 drops
Sandalwood 3 drops

Lemon 6 drops
Ylang Ylang 3 drops
Cedarwood 3 drops

Clary Sage 3 drops
Orange 3 drops
Lavender 3 drops

Bath soaps, candles, cosmetics, and massage oils
can be bought already impregnated with aromatherapy oils.
For therapeutic effect, ensure quality essential oils,
not just fragrant oils, have been used.

Inhalations

One effective way of using essential oils is in an aromatherapy inhalation. Fill a bowl with very hot water, add 6 to 10 drops of suitable oils (see below) and, holding a towel over your head, breathe in the fragrance-filled steam. Breathing in essential oils can help relieve mental fatigue and aid in maintaining a relaxed, clear mind. You can use a towel and a bowl of water (see above) or, for a quicker alternative, saturate a cloth with very hot water and add 1 to 3 drops of an essential oil. Hold the cloth against your face and breathe deeply two or three times. Try 1 drop of lavender and 1 drop of neroli as a calming inhalation, or 2 drops of bergamot and 1 drop of cypress as a pick-me-up.

Vaporizers

Vaporizers, also known as fragrancers, burners, aroma lamps and diffusers, can fill the air with fragrance which will assist you in remaining relaxed and focused throughout your day. Choose one with a reasonably deep "well" if you are planning to burn oils for a few hours, as it is important always to have some water in the bowl.

After filling the bowl of the vaporizer with water, add 3 to 10 drops of essential oil and place a candle underneath the bowl. Check the water level occasionally and top off as needed. One suggestion for a day when you need to be mentally focused is a blend of 6 drops of lemon, 3 drops of rosemary, and 3 drops of basil.

Foot baths

Using warm to hot water in a large bowl, add 4 to 8 drops of essential oils. Soak feet for 15 minutes. This can also be a perfect time to meditate or use some auto-suggestions to relax more deeply (see ATTITUDE, page 34 and MEDITATION, page 64).

A NOTE OF CAUTION

Essential oils are pure and concentrated. Except for lavender and tea tree, the oils should not be applied undiluted to the skin. While most oils are safe to use, some (including basil, cedarwood, clary sage, hyssop, juniper, marjoram, pennyroyal, sage and thyme) should be avoided during pregnancy. Other oils (such as bergamot and lemon) are phototoxic and should not be used on the skin when it is exposed to sunlight. If you are unsure of the use of any oil, or are prone to allergic reactions, are pregnant, or suffer from high blood pressure, epilepsy or another neural disorder, it is best to consult a professional aromatherapist and medical practitioner before use.

Compresses

Cold compresses are very useful in relieving headaches caused by tension and stress. Fill a bowl with ice cold water, add 6 to 10 drops of essential oil and disperse through the water. Place a cloth in the water, then wring out the excess. Place on the forehead and temples for about 20 minutes. Lavender oil works effectively or try a combination, such as 4 drops of lavender, 2 drops of orange, and 2 drops of chamomile.

Aromatherapy pillows

For a sleep pillow, mix dried lavender flowers and dried rose petals, then add 4 drops of cedarwood and 2 drops of orange essential oils. Use this mix to fill a drawstring bag made from cheesecloth, muslin, or thin cotton. Place this "pillow" between your usual pillow and pillowcase. These relaxing oils should help induce a restful and fragrant sleep.

For an eye pillow, cut two pieces of cotton material, each approximately 10 inches (25 cm) long and 4 inches (10 cm) wide. Sew the two rectangles together on three sides. Turn this inside out to make a pouch, and fill with linseed (available from health food stores). Add 2 drops of bergamot, 1 drop of lavender, and 1 drop of orange essential oils. Sew the pouch closed.

Drape this pillow across your eyes when you are relaxing. It can also be placed across your forehead to soothe a tension headache.

Aromatherapy massage

An aromatherapy massage from a qualified aromatherapist is an indulgent relaxation technique that will leave you feeling pampered and nurtured. Your muscles are relaxed, your circulation is improved by the massage, and the essential oils are absorbed through the skin. A professional aromatherapist will consult with you and blend a combination of oils specific to your situation; however, it is also possible for you to use essential oils when you are giving yourself a massage (see MASSAGE, page 56). Use a good quality oil, like sweet almond or avocado, as a "carrier" oil to which you can add a few drops of essential oils.

Attitude

An effective way to develop a more relaxed, calm, and peaceful lifestyle is to become aware of our attitudes and beliefs, and how these relate to the way we deal with stress and stressful events.

If we analyze our reactions, we will see that we don't always act rationally. Often we act on well-established, but inappropriate, beliefs. For example, on an intellectual level we may know that if we make a mistake it is better to face up to it immediately, take responsibility, and deal with the consequences. People who avoid taking responsibility, who attempt to hide the problem or push the blame onto someone else, create situations fraught with fear, anxiety, and guilt that span days instead of an awkward half hour.

Recognizing the beliefs behind our actions is the first step in changing the way we behave. When faced with a potentially stressful situation, you should try to distance yourself from the event for a moment. Ask yourself what action you need to take to deal with the event effectively, and remain focused and relaxed. By accepting that we have a choice to be stressed or relaxed, we give ourselves the power to choose to remain calm.

There are a variety of techniques you can employ to change your attitudes, improve your ability to relax quickly and easily, and to remain calm, avoiding frequent stress.

*Just as our emotional and mental states can be
the cause of stress, our minds and our imaginations
can be the source of healing, peace and relaxation.*

Making choices

For many people the list of things they "must" or "should" do creates enough pressure to keep them constantly stressed. If you feel this applies to you, try a simple technique to reduce stress. Firstly, acknowledge you have choice in whether or not you will do something. This alone can relieve the feeling of being weighed down by demands made on you. Then try saying, "I choose to..." rather than "I must..." or say, "I want to..." rather than "I should..."

When you make a conscious choice to complete tasks, you become motivated to do so. This also includes learning to say "no" when you are asked to do something you feel is outside your responsibilities or which will place unreasonable demands on your time. Saying "yes" when you want to say "no" is likely to make you resentful and angry, and is unlikely to reduce your stress levels. If you generally say "yes" to any request, those around you may initially react to your refusals; however, if you keep calm and polite, they will gradually come to respect your redefined boundaries.

Visualization

A very simple and effective relaxation technique, visualization is, in simple terms, conscious day-dreaming. As you practice visualization, these daydreams will become more vivid, and the time it takes you to achieve relaxation will become shorter.

Our imaginations are powerful tools. Just as we can work our bodies into a "fight or flight" response by thinking about a stressful incident, we can also create a state of deep relaxation by thinking about a calm and peaceful situation.

Visualization can counter negative thoughts, anxiety and nervousness. This process of creating scenarios in our minds, in which we react as we would like to react, can assist in building confidence to deal with challenges; it also provides alternative ways to cope with recurring events that we find stressful.

A visualization
for deep relaxation

Relaxation visualization is effective only if its images are relaxing to you. The following is an example only; the most effective visualizations will be the ones you develop yourself.

When you begin to practice visualization, choose a quiet place where you are unlikely to be disturbed, close your eyes, and take a few deep breaths. Once you become more familiar with the techniques, you will find that noises and interruptions become less of a distraction.

Imagine yourself on a white sandy beach, the day clear and warm. You are wearing loose cotton clothing and lying on a thick towel on the sand. Be aware of how the towel feels against your skin and the difference between this texture and that of the clothing touching your skin. In this vivid mental image, place your hands on your thighs and feel how warm they are from the sun's rays.

Appreciate the vibrant colors of the sea and sky and their contrast with the silvery white of the sand. Run your fingers through the sand beside you and feel how the top layer is fine, warm and dry; while the layer of sand below is cooler and slightly damp. See and feel how some of the grains of sand cling to your hands. Smell the seaweed drying on the beach and taste the slightly salty air. Hear the rhythmic sound of the waves breaking on the beach. Be aware of how completely mentally and physically relaxed you are in this image.

A visualization for a stressful situation

If there is an event approaching that you feel nervous and anxious about, it will help to develop a visualization about this event. The length of time it takes to do this will depend on how stressful the event is to you. You may like to come back to it on a few occasions until you can complete the visualization from beginning to end, without feeling stressed.

Again, try to incorporate taste, touch, smell, sound, and vision into the visualization. Begin with images just before the anticipated event. In your mind's eye, see the room around you. Visualize the clothes you are wearing, and feel the sensations created by the fabric on your body. Become conscious of the smells in the room. Hear the sounds in the room and those that are coming from outside.

Once this visualization is clear in your mind, slowly increase the visualization to include every step toward the event, including all moments that are causing you, or will cause you, concern.

If at any time you are not progressing as you would like to or negative mind-chatter begins to creep in, simply stop and begin again at whichever point you feel comfortable. If you begin to feel anxious, distance yourself from the image for a moment and take a few deep breaths. You may decide to finish the session at this point or begin again once you have relaxed.

AUTO-SUGGESTION
AND AFFIRMATIONS

*Auto-suggestions and affirmations can be used
with other relaxation techniques, such as during a bath
or while practicing meditation or breathing exercises.*

Auto-suggestion and affirmations both work on the verbal or mental
repetition of a positive phrase that states — as though it is fact — your
situation as you would like to experience it.

The emphasis in auto-suggestion is to repeat the phrase while in a deeply
relaxed state, thus allowing the subconscious mind to absorb the meaning
of the phrase and create change in behavioral and belief patterns.

The principle of affirmations is based on the concept that you create your
own environment by how you think. You are therefore more likely to
achieve your goals if you think positively than if you dwell on the negative.
Affirmations can be used at any time, whether you are deeply relaxed or not.
They also act as reminders of your goals or your desired states of being.

To be effective, the phrases you use should be:

- specific — contemplate what it is you want

- in the present tense

- in the first person — use "I"

- positive — state what you want, not what you don't want

- repeated — either in your mind, audibly, or
by writing it down.

Examples of affirmations/auto-suggestions for relaxation include:

- "I remain relaxed and calm throughout the day."

- "I choose to work in a relaxed and peaceful manner."

- "I am more than capable of dealing with today's challenges."

- "I am confident and relaxed."

- "I am calm, cool and collected."

Breathing Techniques

Breathing is fundamental to our health. Apart from the obvious fact that it is impossible for us to live without breathing, the way we breathe can have dramatic effects on the way our bodies operate and the way we feel.

When we inhale, we are taking air into our lungs; the blood vessels in the lungs absorb the oxygen that the blood transports around the body. At the same time, the blood releases carbon dioxide into the air within the lungs, and this waste product is then exhaled. The balance of oxygen absorbed and carbon dioxide expelled is the key to effective breathing. Shallow breathing can result in too little oxygen being absorbed, thus depriving the cells in our bodies of oxygen and leaving a surplus of carbon dioxide in the lung tissue. Hyperventilation can cause the body to expel too much carbon dioxide, producing dizziness, sweating, and palpitations. This often leads to increased anxiety and results in even faster breathing, worsening the effects.

The good news is that learning to breathe properly is not difficult, although it will take practice before it becomes your automatic breathing pattern.

Breathing is one of the most effective and most practical relaxation and calming techniques. Once you are familiar with the exercises, they can be practiced quickly and effectively at any time, even if you only have a few minutes to spare.

*By placing your hands on your abdomen as you breathe,
you will be able to feel your abdomen expand,
causing your hands to move outward. Effective breathing
comes from the diaphram, not the chest.*

Deep breathing exercise

It is easiest to first practice correct breathing lying down. Once you have
become comfortable with the technique you will be able to use it
standing, sitting, or when walking and exercising. Remove any tight or
uncomfortable clothing and support your head with a rolled towel, making
sure the support is not too high and keeping your airways straight.

1. Place your hands at the bottom of your rib cage. This keeps your
attention on how you are breathing. It may take a few breaths before you
feel comfortable with this technique, so don't become anxious and
concerned about doing it right the first time. If you become lightheaded
return to your normal breathing for a few moments then try again.

Step 1

2. Inhale through your nose and, breathing slowly and deeply, try to fill your abdominal cavity with air. Try not to move your shoulders or puff out your chest.

3. Exhale through your mouth and feel your abdominal muscles fall. If you also feel your shoulders fall, it means that you lifted them while inhaling. Be aware of this and try not to lift them with your next breath.

4. Repeat this step several times until you feel comfortable with the rhythm. On each exhalation, imagine all the tension in your body leaving with your breath.

5. Finish by returning to a normal depth of breathing, but try to maintain the style of breathing. Rise slowly.

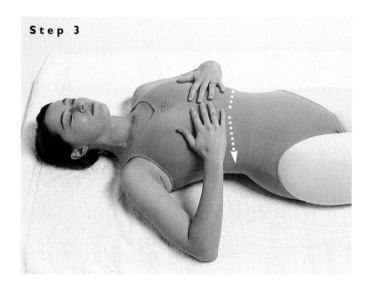

Step 3

Exhalation exercise

This is a different type of exercise because, rather than focusing on breathing in, it concentrates on expelling as much air as possible during exhalation; thus inhalation becomes a reflex action. It is also a useful exercise to relieve stress as the movement of your body helps release physical and emotional tensions.

1. Stand with your feet shoulder-width apart and arms hanging loosely by your sides. Bring your arms up in front of you as you take in a deep breath.

2. Make a loud "haaaa" or "oooo" sound and, at the same time, bend your knees and allow your upper body to become limp and flop over, your head ending up near your knees. As the top half of your body falls forward, your arms should swing down freely. Expel as much air as possible, repeating the "haaaa" or "oooo" sound if necessary.

3. Take in a deep breath as you slowly rise back to a standing position.

4. Take two or three normal breaths so that you don't get dizzy, and then repeat.

Sectional breathing exercise

This exercise will further increase your awareness of how you breathe. Once you have become familiar with this exercise you will find it useful as an almost instant stress reliever. On a long-term basis, this exercise can improve your digestion, reduce muscular tension in the shoulder and neck areas, and increase your lung capacity.

1. Place your hands over your lower abdomen. Breathe slowly in through your nose, focusing on filling your lower abdomen and pelvic area with air. Exhale slowly and as fully as possible through your mouth.

2. Repeat this for another six breaths.

3. Move your hands to the lower half of your rib cage. Make sure your shoulders are relaxed and take seven breaths in through your nose and out through your mouth, focusing on expanding your rib cage with every inhalation.

4. Rest your fingers on your collar bone (see opposite). Focusing on expanding the upper chest and shoulder area, without moving your shoulders upwards, take seven deep breaths in through the nose and out through the mouth.

5. Now take seven long, deep breaths and fill all three areas with each breath, then feel these areas contract as you exhale.

6. Return to normal breathing and remain seated for a few minutes.

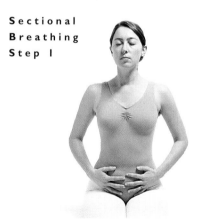

Sectional Breathing Step 1

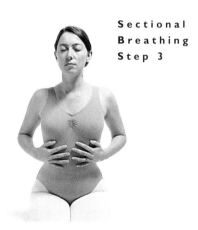

Sectional Breathing Step 3

Color

The colors that surround us and those that we wear can have a significant impact on the way we feel.

The colors around us have psychological and physical effects, and can influence our emotions, our stress levels, our blood pressure, and the way in which we perceive our environment. They can be used to help us feel more relaxed, increase our ability to focus, or feel more energetic.

As a rule, paler shades of a color will be more relaxing than darker shades when used for interiors. Dark shades can become oppressive and reduce the perceived amount of space in a room. Even in clothes, white and very pale shades are believed by many to be the most effective for relaxation.

Experiment wearing different colors, taking notice of how you feel when you are wearing each one. For a start, try imagining yourself wearing a bright red shirt on a bleak, overcast day. How does it make you feel? Now imagine yourself wearing the same bright red shirt in the worst heat and humidity. No doubt you've experienced contrasting reactions to each scenario — it is important to dress to suit your moods and energy levels.

Red is stimulating and increases the appetite — a good choice for a kitchen, but not for a room in which you would like to relax or sleep. Red has been shown to increase blood pressure. It can be helpful in lifting spirits.

Orange has similar qualities to red. It is stimulating, it increases the appetite, and can also help to create warmth.

Yellow is emotionally uplifting. It helps us concentrate and stimulates the mind, making it perfect when incorporated into an office or workroom, but not into a bedroom.

Green has soothing qualities, which make it suitable for most rooms. Wearing green can be calming on days when you feel stressed or anxious.

Blue is gentle and relaxing, and creates a feeling of space. Blue will give a room a calming atmosphere; it has the opposite effect to red and can be used to lower blood pressure. Pale blue is a wonderful choice for a bedroom.

Pale purple and lavenders create a peaceful, relaxing feeling. Darker shades of purple are also restful, but should be used in smaller amounts as they can become depressing. Because purple contains red, it can also add warmth to an area.

Used in excess black can be overpowering and depressing. Business people often wear black to promote an impression of power and control.

White creates a feeling of space and peace, but can give a room a cold, clinical feeling. Wearing white helps you to be relaxed and alert at the same time.

Exercise

Regular exercise is vital to maintaining a healthy and relaxed lifestyle. It does not need to be vigorous or strenuous exercise, and it is always wise to begin with a little and gradually build — but it does need to be regular.

If you haven't exercised for a long time, choose a gentle form of exercise that you know will fit easily with your routine. As you feel the benefits, and doing more becomes easier, try to vary the type of exercise you do. This will not only stop you from getting bored with the routine, but will also enable you to exercise different muscle groups.

Walking

Walking is an ideal form of exercise as it doesn't matter what your fitness level is when you begin. It is also gentle on your joints, although a good pair of sport shoes is essential to protect your knees, ankles, and lower back from undue strain. Start with a pace and distance that are comfortable for you, and gradually increase both so that you are doing a little more each day.

Dancing

If you can allow yourself to dance without inhibition, it can be a very effective means of self-expression and relaxation. Choose music you enjoy and that suits your mood or purpose. Begin with smooth, slow movements until your muscles have had a chance to warm up, then move in whatever way feels right for you.

Stretching

Stretching is a must before beginning any sort of exercise; it can also be beneficial as an exercise routine to reduce stress and tension, and to promote relaxation. Stretching, as part of a regular routine, will improve your flexibility, strength, and stamina; it improves circulation and helps your body eliminate waste products more effectively. Develop a routine and try to practice it every day as part of your relaxation program.

Eye excercise

Shifting Focus

Focus your vision on an object 1 to 2 feet (30 to 60 cm) away and hold for about a minute. Now shift your focus to an object approximately 20 feet (7 m) away and hold for a minute. Repeat three or four times. This is an excellent exercise if you do a lot of close-up work or if you work on a computer. Ideally, put this exercise into practice once an hour while you are working — also use this time to take a few deep breaths.

Palming

Cup the palms of your hands over your eyes with your fingertips lying in a cross on your forehead so that your eyes are in complete darkness. Keep your eyes open and leave your hands in place for at least five minutes. Breathe deeply and slowly during this process. Colors may appear to be brighter and more vibrant after your eyes have rested.

Stretching exercise

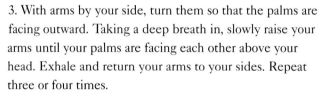

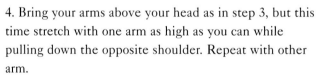

1. Begin each session by standing with your feet shoulder-width apart, knees very slightly bent, arms hanging loosely by your side and torso straight. Make sure your weight is evenly distributed over your legs.

2. Straighten your legs and lock your knees; lift one leg up and flex your toes back toward your leg, then point them away from you. Repeat three or four times. Then, gently and slowly, rotate your foot around the ankle. Repeat three or four times. Repeat this step with your other foot.

3. With arms by your side, turn them so that the palms are facing outward. Taking a deep breath in, slowly raise your arms until your palms are facing each other above your head. Exhale and return your arms to your sides. Repeat three or four times.

4. Bring your arms above your head as in step 3, but this time stretch with one arm as high as you can while pulling down the opposite shoulder. Repeat with other arm.

5. To stretch your right side, widen your stance slightly and, breathing in, let your left hand slide down the length of your leg while you bring your right arm up and over your head. Exhale and return your right arm to your side. Repeat this exercise stretching your left side.

6. Repeat steps 4 and 5 three or four times.

7. Keeping your stance wide, bend your knees and balance your upper body over your hips. With palms facing inward, inhale and raise your arms to shoulder height.

Step 7

8. Exhale as you bring your hands in front of your chest, keeping arms at shoulder level. As you inhale, twist your upper body at the waist, first to the right, leading with the right arm.

9. Return to center and exhale, then inhale as you repeat, twisting to the left, leading with the left arm. Return to the center and exhale. Inhale as you move your hands out again, and exhale as you lower your arms to your sides.

Step 8

10. Repeat steps 8 and 9 three or four times.

11. Stand with feet shoulder-width apart with your right foot facing forward and your left foot at a right angle to your right foot. With your right foot, take a large step forward and bend your knee. While keeping your upper body straight and your weight evenly distributed over your hips, you should be able to feel the stretch along your inner thigh.

12. Repeat step 11 using your left leg.

Step 11

Herbs

Herbal preparations are available commercially in many forms, from teabags to tinctures, tablets to tonics. They may contain a single herb or a combination that has been blended to treat a particular condition.

Throughout the ages, almost every culture in the world has had a tradition of using plants for health and healing. Texts detailing the use of herbs as medicine have been discovered from the ancient civilizations in Egypt and the Middle East, Greece, Rome, and China. The study of plants and their therapeutic use continues to develop and expand today, as scientific research combines with knowledge collected and recorded over centuries. Like many natural therapies, the aim of herbal medicine is to put the body back into balance and allow it to heal itself.

Though the principles of herbal medicine are concerned with healing over a period of time, herbal remedies will often have quite rapid and noticeable effects on the symptoms of a condition. For specific health problems, a herbal medicine practitioner should be consulted; there are, however, many herbal remedies effective in reducing stress, which are as easy to use as making a cup of tea.

Tinctures

Tinctures are created by steeping herbs, often for weeks, in pure or diluted alcohol. A small quantity of the tincture will then be further diluted and taken two or three times per day with meals. Most people choose to buy commercially prepared tinctures or else obtain them from a herbal medicine practitioner. In either case, the recommendations given for quantity and frequency of dose should be strictly observed.

❦ *Echinacea* — is a herb that assists the body's immune system in fighting infections. This is a suitable herb to take if you have been under stress for a long period of time, feel run down, and seem to be more susceptible to minor infections, such as colds or blemished skin.

❦ *Marigold* — is beneficial in the treatment of anxiety and digestive complaints. This herb is also known as calendula.

Inhalations

Inhalations are prepared by placing fresh herbs in a large bowl and pouring on near-boiling water. Place your face over the bowl with a towel over your head to form a tent, and breathe in the fragrant steam.

❦ *Sweet basil* — can calm nervousness and may be useful if you are not sleeping well.

❦ *Lavender* — makes a beautifully calming inhalation. Crush the fresh flowers before adding the water.

Infusions and teas

Teas are made by steeping the leaves, flowers, fruit, stems, or seeds of a plant in boiling water for a few minutes. An infusion is generally much stronger than a tea and is made by steeping the herbs in hot or cold oil or water for anything from a few minutes to weeks.

❦ *Chamomile* — is useful for the relief of tension headaches; it is also a relaxing drink before bed. Adding the strained tea to a hot bath will help relax muscles and reduce fatigue.

❦ *Valerian root* — is very effective if stress is preventing you from sleeping soundly, as valerian tea acts to soothe the nervous system. This herb has a rather unpleasant taste, so a teaspoon of dried valerian root powder is generally mixed into a cup of warm milk. A teaspoon of honey may also help to make the tea more palatable.
Caution: Valerian is a powerful herb and should not be used in large amounts or over long periods of time, unless on advice from a qualified herbal medicine practitioner.

❦ *Lavender* — is an infusion of lavender leaves and acts as a gentle sedative. Try this if you are anxious or having difficulty sleeping.

❦ *Peppermint* — is beneficial before bedtime, and for the relief of headaches and digestive problems.

❦ *St John's wort* — relaxes and will leave you feeling refreshed.

❦ *Thyme* — reduces tension and relieves headaches.

❦ *Skullcap* — helps reduce stress and relieve headaches, promotes sleep, and acts as a general tonic for the nervous system. Honey is often added to balance the bitter taste. This herb should not be taken in large quantities.

Compresses

To make a cold compress, take a clean cotton cloth and dip it into a cooled infusion or diluted tincture of your selected herbs. Wring the cloth and then place it directly onto the skin. It is time to replenish the cloth with the infusion when the cloth warms to body temperature.

❧ *Borage* — compresses made from the leaves of this herb are effective in reducing tiredness in the legs caused by too much standing.

❧ *Chamomile* — compresses made from chamomile flowers will help relieve tired and strained eyes. For best results, lie on your back with the compress over your eyes and breathe deeply.

❧ *Rosemary* — provides effective relief from tension headaches. Use an infusion of fresh rosemary leaves or the essential oil, place the compress across your brow and down onto your temples.

❧ *Peppermint* — provides relief from headaches. Use an infusion of peppermint leaves or the essential oil. Place the compress on your brow and temples.

Relaxing Massage

One of our instinctive reactions to pain or injury is to touch the area; we rub a sore joint and stroke the hand of someone in pain. Massage is an extension of this desire to touch and be touched, utilizing a range of different strokes and techniques.

While giving yourself a massage is not as luxurious as receiving a massage from someone else, it is an effective and enjoyable relaxation technique. One benefit of self-massage is that you can feel where you want to focus most attention and feel when one area has had enough massage. You may choose to undress for a self-massage if time and privacy permit, and make use of a good massage oil such as avocado or sweet almond oil or a blend of essential oils. If you choose not to undress, loosen or remove any tight-fitting clothing.

The benefits of massage

• Improved circulation • More efficient digestion

• Faster elimination of waste products • Relaxation of muscles and of the central

nervous system • Mental clarity • General feeling of well-being and calm

Preparation

Do your best to ensure you will be comfortable throughout the massage. The room should be pleasantly warm but not hot; dimmed lighting or candlelight and some soft, relaxing music help create a nurturing and peaceful atmosphere. If you are undressing for the massage have plenty of towels available to drape over the parts of your body you're not working on, otherwise you may feel the cold more as you relax. Try to ensure you won't be disturbed. Two of the most important elements in a good self-massage are breathing and rhythm, so begin by making sure you are comfortable and take a few moments to focus on your breathing. If deep relaxation is your goal, use long, slow strokes.

Do not worry about being expert in massage techniques. What's important is the touch of skin on skin, the time you spend on yourself, and the calm thoughts.

Massage movements

Stroking

Long, gentle strokes using both hands simultaneously or alternating.

Effleurage

Long, even strokes using firm pressure in one direction, and light pressure in the opposite direction (on arms and legs, firm pressure should always be used toward the heart). Keep contact with your body between the strokes.

Petrissage

A rhythmic, kneading movement with one hand holding and squeezing, while the other hand releases. Particularly useful on the fleshy parts of the body.

Frictions

Small, circular movements made with the pads of the thumbs or fingers. Use this movement to work on areas that feel tight.

When you are massaging yourself, try to clear your mind and focus on the sensation alone. It is important to be comfortable and to keep all your muscles relaxed.

Neck, shoulders and arms

Sit on the floor or in a chair, or lie with your back on the floor, your knees bent and your feet flat on the floor.

1. Using your right hand, stroke from the bottom of your skull, down the left side of your neck to your shoulder, over your shoulder and down your arm to the elbow. Glide your hand gently back to the base of your skull and repeat two or three times.

2. With your right hand, use gentle kneading movements and work from the left side of your neck down to your left wrist. Gently glide your hand back to your neck and repeat.

3. Use circular friction movements to work more deeply into the muscles. Begin at the back of your neck, beside the spine, and work out to the side of the neck, and down to your left shoulder. Glide your right hand to your left wrist and work up your forearm to your elbow with circular frictions.

4. Repeat steps 1 to 3 using your left hand on the right side of your body.

Face and scalp

A face and scalp massage alone can help relieve tension headaches, increase your energy level and help improve your circulation, thus improving your appearance. It is worth using a very small amount of good quality light oil or a little moisturizer so you don't stretch the skin of your face. This routine can be carried out lying down or seated.

1. Place both hands at the base of your skull, your fingertips meeting in the middle. Using small, circular frictions, gradually work your way to the sides of your head, just behind the ears. You may like to pay more attention to any spots that feel tender or tight.

Step 1

2. Gradually work your way upward, continuing with the frictions until your hands meet at the top of your head. Then massage the whole of your scalp in this way.

3. Place both hands over your eyes with your fingers on your forehead and the heels of your hands on your cheeks. Spend a few moments like this breathing deeply.

4. Stroke along the sides of your nose, along your cheekbones to your ears. Run your fingertips down along the jaw line until your hands meet at your chin. Repeat two or three times.

5. Gently knead along the jaw line from your chin to your ears. Then gently knead your ears upward from the lobes.

6. With very light, circular movements, massage all around the mouth, cheeks, the sides of the nose, and the eyes. Stroke over the eyebrows and down around the top of your cheekbone with your middle finger until you reach the top of your nose.

7. Apply gentle pressure to the inside of the eye socket and hold for several seconds.

8. Using your fingertips, stroke upward from the bridge of your nose to the top of your forehead. Repeat this several times.

9. Now massage with both hands, using small, circular movements from the bridge of your nose to your hairline, then down to your temples.

10. Finish your massage with extremely light stroking all over your face, and take a few deep breaths before gently proceeding with your day.

Step 6

Legs and feet

Sit on the floor with one leg extended in front of you and the other bent at the knee so you can hold your foot. Work on one entire leg first and then repeat the steps with your other leg.

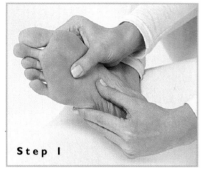

Step 1

1. Holding the top of your foot with one hand, use firm strokes along the sole of your foot from toes to ankle. Glide hand back to toes and repeat three or four times.

2. Gently roll each toe between your thumb and first finger, and then give each toe a gentle pull.

3. Using both thumbs and firm pressure, work with small, circular movements from the ankle to the toes, covering all of the sole. Repeat step 1.

4. Bend the knee of the leg you have been working on and, starting from the instep, stroke both hands up the shin, over the knee and up the length of your thigh. Repeat this stroke two to three times.

5. With your knee still bent, draw both hands up from your ankle, and up the back of your leg. Repeat two to three times.

6. Using a kneading movement, work on the back of your leg, first around your calf muscle and then on the back of your thigh. Don't knead your knee; instead use a light gentle movement around the kneecap.

7. Knead the top and sides of your thigh. Then use small, circular movements on any place that feels tight.

Step 6

Abdomen and chest

Lie on your back with a towel or pillow supporting your head, knees bent and feet flat on the floor.

1. With one hand over the other, stroke in a clockwise direction around your abdomen.

2. Using a gentle, plucking movement with thumb and index fingers, lift the flesh of the abdominal area.

3. Next, hold your right hand flat against your lower abdomen, pull your hand up firmly toward the bottom of the rib cage, turn your hand so that your fingers point across your body, and push across to the left hand side, then push down firmly with the heel of the hand from the rib cage to the lower abdomen. This movement assists the digestive process, which can become sluggish when we are stressed.

4. Move your hands to the center of your collarbone, and gently stroke from the center out to the shoulders using your fingertips.

5. Follow this with gentle, circular frictions around the chest and under the collarbone. Then repeat step 4.

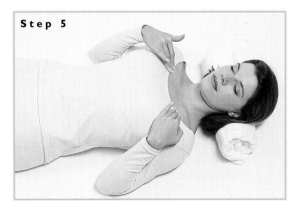

At the end of this sequence you will feel calm, peaceful and relaxed.

Meditation

Meditation can take you into a state where your body is completely relaxed and your mind is alert, yet still and peaceful. Benefits associated with regular practice of meditation are clarity of mind, mental alertness, improved creativity, the ability to concentrate for longer periods of time, and improved coordination.

Like most things, meditation improves with practice. Start by meditating for just a few minutes, gradually increasing the length of time. Try to make a regular time each day for meditation and persevere. Some people find it most convenient to meditate in the morning when they are alert, while others find that meditation can encourage sound sleep. There are many different ways to meditate, so experiment to find which one is most suitable for you.

Preparation

Find a quiet place that is free from distractions. Before you begin the meditation, ensure you are comfortable — wear loose clothing and make sure you are warm. There are a variety of positions you can try, but whichever one you use, it is important that your spine remains straight.

Meditation positions

• Sitting on the ground cross-legged. You may like to support your back against a wall.

• Sitting in a straight-backed chair with hands lying loosely in your lap, palms facing upward.

• Lying on your back. If you feel you may fall asleep, try another position.

• Lotus or half-lotus position (if this is comfortable).

• Kneeling position with hands resting face up on the thighs. A meditation stool will make this more comfortable.

Focusing on the breath

Begin by taking very deep, smooth breaths. As thoughts move into your mind, do not attempt to get rid of them. Instead, try to be an observer to your thoughts. Don't judge them as right or wrong, silly or distracting, just allow them to come and go without becoming emotionally involved or allowing them to develop. Then consciously return your focus to your breath.

Focusing on an object

Light a candle or choose a small, beautiful object like a single flower, a shell, or a piece of stone or crystal. Place this object at eye level, 1 to 2 feet (30 to 60 cm) away from you. Settle into your chosen position and begin to breathe deeply and evenly, focusing your attention on the object. As thoughts enter your mind, observe them objectively and without judgment, and bring your focus back to the object.

Using a mantra

A mantra is a word or phrase that is repeated, either audibly or silently, over and over again as a way of concentrating the mind. If you are meditating for relaxation, choose a word or phrase that has a positive meaning for you and repeat this as you keep your breathing in a slow, even rhythm.

Guided meditations

If you have difficulty meditating, you may like to try one of the many guided meditation audio cassettes available. These will lead you through a process that will assist you in focusing on your breath and on relaxing parts of your body. You may also like to make your own guide by reading onto a tape while you play soothing music in the background. Begin with instructions to focus on your breath followed by instructions to relax all parts of your body, starting at your toes and working your way up to your scalp. Speak slowly, smoothly and with clarity.

Music

People respond to music on a highly individual level. What one person may find relaxing and soothing, another may find boring or irritating. When we hear a piece of music we may recall the emotional experiences of other times we heard that music. There are, however, particular pieces of music that are likely to assist you in achieving a relaxed state.

When choosing music for relaxation, it is important to establish what you want to achieve. Do you want to reach a state of deep relaxation? Or do you wish to focus while you work or study? Perhaps you need a boost of energy.

Music whose tempo is faster than our resting heartbeat will often have the effect of increasing our heart rate, breathing, and blood pressure. Similarly, music with a slower tempo can assist in lowering them.

To relax deeply, music with a slow tempo and even rhythm is most effective. Much of the new music written for relaxation utilizes long, sustained notes and may incorporate sounds from nature such as bird song.

Pieces for solo instruments, two instruments, or for small chamber groups help the mind focus. Most music of the Baroque period is useful for this purpose. Energizing music will generally have a faster pace and may be more complex in its instrumentation.

When using music to remain calm
or for relaxation, the volume should not be too high
as loud sounds are stressful to the body.

Calming and soothing music

From the Baroque period

- Canon in D by Pachelbel (violins and basso continuo)
- Adagio in G minor by Albinoni (strings and organ)

From the Classical period

- "Laudate Dominum" aria from *Vesperae solennes de confessore*, K339 by Mozart (soprano and orchestra)
- Slow movements from Piano Concertos Nos. 20, 21, 23, 24 by Mozart
- Clarinet Concerto in A, 2nd movement, by Mozart
- Piano Sonata Op. 27 No. 2, 1st movement, by Beethoven ("Moonlight")
- Symphony No. 7, slow movement, by Beethoven

From the Romantic period

- The complete Nocturnes by Chopin (piano solo)
- Piano Quintet in A Op. 81 by Dvorak (piano and string quartet)
- Largo from Symphony No. 9 in E minor Op. 95 by Dvorak ("From The New World")

From the French Impressionists and early 20th century

- *La Mer* by Debussy (orchestral)
- *Deux Arabesques* Nos. 1 & 2 by Ravel (piano solo)
- "Clair de Lune" from *Suite bergamasque* by Debussy (piano solo)
- *Pavane for a Dead Princess* by Ravel (orchestral or piano version)
- Arrangements for flute and harp of pieces by Debussy, Ravel, Faure, and others
- *Fantasia on a Theme of Thomas Tallis* by Vaughan Williams (orchestral)

Energizing and uplifting music

From the Baroque period

- *The Four Seasons* by Vivaldi (violin with stringed orchestra)
- Chorus: (68) "Wir setzen uns mit Tranen nieder"
  from *St Matthew Passion* by J.S. Bach

From the Classical period

- Piano concertos by Mozart
- 3rd movement, Piano Sonata Op. 27 No. 2 by Beethoven ("Moonlight")
- 1st movement from Piano Sonata Op. 13 by Beethoven ("Pathetique")
- Piano Sonata Op. 57 by Beethoven ("Appassionata")
- Piano Sonata Op. 53 by Beethoven ("Walstein")
- Piano Sonata Op. 31 No. 2 by Beethoven ("Tempest")
- Symphony No. 9 by Beethoven ("Choral")
- Piano Concertos Nos 1, 3, 4, 5 by Beethoven
- Piano Trio in E Flat D.929 Op. 100 by Schubert (piano, violin, cello)

From the Romantic period

- Ballades by Chopin (piano solo)
- Polonaises by Chopin (piano solo)
- *Rhapsody on a Theme of Paganini* by Rachmaninov
  (for piano and orchestra)
- Piano Concerto No. 2 by Rachmaninov

From the French Impressionists and early 20th century

- 1st and 3rd movements from *Sonatine* by Ravel (piano solo)
- Piano Concerto No. 3 by Prokofiev

Focusing music

• Gregorian Chants (Abbey of Solesmes, France is recommended)

From the Baroque period

• *Goldberg Variations* by J.S. Bach (piano or harpsichord)

• *The Well-Tempered Clavier* Books I and II by J.S. Bach (piano or harpsichord)

• Suites for cello solo by J.S. Bach, esp. No. 3 in C

• *Brandenburg concertos* by J.S. Bach esp. No. 3 (strings)

• Sonatas for Viola da Gamba and Keyboard by J.S. Bach esp. 2nd movement BWV 1029

• Sonatas for Violin and Keyboard by J.S. Bach

• *Water Music* by Handel (orchestral)

• Music for harpischord by Handel

• Suite in A minor for Recorder and Strings by Telemann

From the Classical period

• Flute Concerto No. 1 in G Major by Mozart

• Piano concertos by Mozart

• Piano Trio in E Flat D.897 by Schubert (Notturno Op. Posth. 148)

From the Romantic period

• Waltzes by Chopin (piano solo)

• *Songs Without Words* for piano by Mendelssohn (piano solo)

• String Quartet No. 12 in F, Op. 96 by Dvorak ("American")

• *Songs of the Auvergne* by Canteloube (soprano and orchestra)

Yoga

Yoga brings harmony to our existence and nurtures our whole being. It is a gentle art involving no strain or great exertion, and can be practiced by anyone, irrespective of age or state of health.

The word "yoga" translates as "union," and the goal of those making yoga their way of life is to unite the mind, body, and spirit. Its benefits are clarity of mind, increased powers of concentration, spiritual awareness, the ability to deeply relax, plus physical strength and flexibility.

Originally from India, yoga is a complex and complete philosophy of life that has developed over thousands of years. It is not necessary, however, to dedicate your life to the practice of yoga to effectively use it as a relaxation technique.

The following "asanas" or exercises can provide a gentle exercise routine, and provide a means for releasing stress and tension. All exercises should be carried out slowly and while observing the suggested breathing.

Wall stand

This position is useful in the relief of tension headaches; it also helps reduce fatigue in the legs. Firstly, sit on the floor, one hip against a wall.

Slowly swing your legs around, one at a time, so they are pointing up, resting against the wall. As part of the same movement, pivot your trunk around and lie down on the floor (use a rolled towel to support your head if necessary).

Make sure that your buttocks are against the wall, and that your upper body is flat and at right angles with your legs, which should be straight.

Relax your arms and feet and hold this position for about 5 minutes (see Position 1). As an alternative position, you may like to spread your legs apart and feel the different muscles this uses (see Position 2).

Position 1

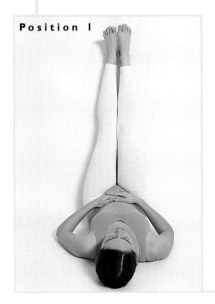

Position 2

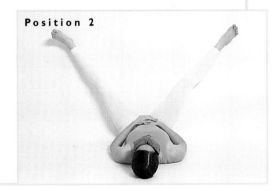

Step 1

Salute to the sun (Surya Namaskar)

Salute to the Sun is a practice composed of 12 successive steps. These 12 positions flow together into one long movement. Salute to the Sun stimulates the muscles, the internal organs, the body systems, and the brain.

Awareness

Concentrate on the breath. Breathe in fully as you stretch and breathe out as you bend. Notice how correct breath gives a smooth movement.

1. Stand straight with your legs and feet together, palms touching in a "prayer" position.

2. Inhale and raise both hands above your head, bend slightly backward from the waist, and tilt your head back.

3. Exhale and slowly bring your upper body forward and down. Place your hands flat on the floor on either side of your feet. (Bend your knees if necessary.)

Step 2

Step 3

Caution: Do not overexert yourself in this practice. Salute to the Sun is very powerful. If you begin to feel weak or dizzy, cease the practice and rest.

Salute to the Sun massages every part of the body — it is a full exercise regime in itself. Practice the Salute first thing in the morning to welcome each new day as a day of calm.

Step 4

4. Inhale, moving your right foot backward, and lower your right knee to the floor. Look upward and arch your back slightly, keeping hips as low as possible.

Step 5

5. Exhale and move the left foot back to join the right, taking the weight of your body on your hands and toes. Your back and arms should be straight.

Step 6

6. Inhale as you slowly lower your knees. Keeping your toes curled, move your buttocks back toward your heels.

Step 7

7. Exhale and move your chest along the floor, keeping hips and buttocks up.

Step 8

8. Inhale and lower your hips to the ground, legs together with the soles of your feet pointing upward, your back arched, shoulders relaxed, and head facing up and back.

Step 9

9. Exhale as you curl your toes under and move your buttocks toward the ceiling, creating an inverted "V" shape. Heels should be on the floor, head should be dropped forward.

Step 10

10. Inhale and move your right foot backward, and drop the right knee as in step 4.

11. Exhale and bring your left foot forward as you bend at the waist, as in step 3.

12. Inhale and take both arms above your head, as in step 2.

13. Exhale as you lower your arms, bringing your palms together, as in step 1.

This sequence of exercise may be repeated, alternating which leg is used first in step 4 and step 10. Take a few deep breaths in "prayer" position before continuing.

Index

Abdominal massage, 63
Acupressure, 24–25
Acupuncture, 24
Affirmations, 38–39
Alcohol, 11
Arm massage, 60
Aroma lamps, 31
Aromatherapy, 27–32
Attitudes, 34–45
Auto-suggestion, 38–39

Basil, 53
Baths
    aromatherapy, 18, 28–29
    foot, 31
Bedtime preparation, 18–19
    aromatherapy bath, 29
Beliefs, effect of, 34
Borage, 54
Brain wave patterns, 7
Breathing techniques, 40–45

Carbon dioxide, 7, 40
Chamomile, 54, 55
Chest massage, 63
Ch'i, 24
Choices, making, 35
Circulation, 7
Clothes, color of, 46
Colors, effects of, 46–48

Compresses
    cold, 32
    herbal, 55
Conception Vessel system, 24

Dancing, 48
Day-dreaming, 35
Deep breathing exercise,
    41–42
Deep relaxation
    effect, 7–8
    exercise, 20–23
    visualization, 36
Desk stretch exercise, 15
Diet, 11
Diffusers, 31

Echinacea, 53
Effleurage, 59
Emotional stress, 11
    calming technique, 17
Environment, impact of, 11
Essential oils, 27
    baths, 28
    safety, 31
Exercises, 48–51
    breathing, 41–45
    deep relaxation, 20–23
    before sleep ,19
    for tension, 13–15
    yoga, 72–77

Exhalation exercise, 43
Eye exercises, 49
Eye pillow, 32

Facial massage, 61
Feet
    baths, 31
    massage, 62
Focusing
    eyes, 49
    meditation, 66
    music, 71
Fragrancers, 31
Frictions (massage), 59

Governing Vessel system,
    24
Guided meditations, 67

Hand acupressure, 25
Head acupressure, 25
Headaches, 32
Herbs, 52–55
Hormones,m 7
Hyperventilation, 40

Infusions, herbal, 54
Inhalations
    aromatherapy, 30
    herbal, 53

This edition first published in Great Britain in 2001 by Aurum Press Ltd
25 Bedford Avenue, London WC1B 3AT

First published by Lansdowne Publishing Pty Ltd
Sydney NSW 2000 Australia

A catalogue reference for this book is available from the British Library.

ISBN 1 85410 813 1

10 9 8 7 6 5 4 3 2 1
2005   2004   2003   2002   2001

Set in Caslon 540 Roman on QuarkXPress
Printed in Singapore by Tien Wah Press (Pte) Ltd